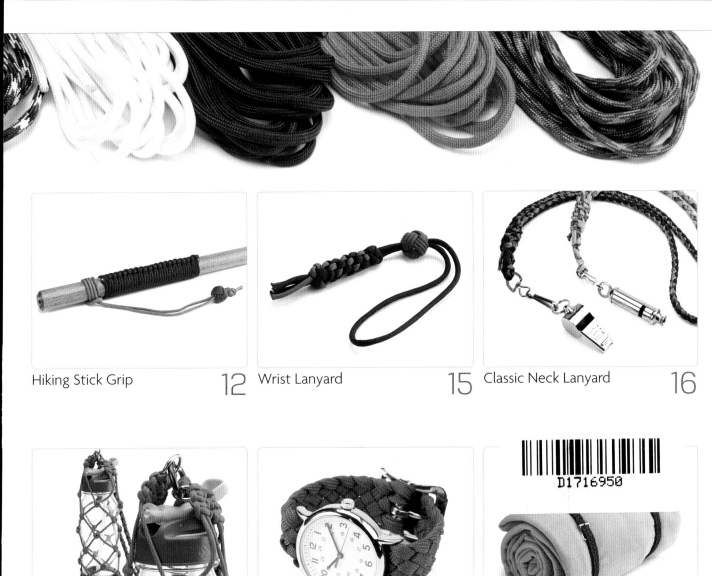

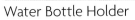

D1716950

INTRODUCTION

In its current form, parachute cord is a product of the Second World War. Historically, silk was used in various lifesaving military applications due to its strength-to-weight ratio. Notable uses were webbed straps, parachute cloth, and shroud lines. After the attack on Pearl Harbor in 1941, however, trade with Japan ended, causing a shortage of silk and the need to find a replacement.

Nylon had been invented about six years earlier by Wallace Carothers at DuPont. The strong, lightweight, and consistent synthetic material actually proved superior to silk when utilized properly. The invention of nylon coupled with the military need for a silk replacement resulted in parachute cord (or paracord).

The military specifications for minimum standards of paracord are outlined by MIL-C-5040H in six types. The most common is Type III (type 3) or 550 parachute cord. The "550" is in reference to the minimum tensile strength specified by the US government. Initially, paracord was only available in olive drab and "natural," an off-white color. Until recently it was a surplus item.

Due to its very high tensile strength, soldiers and sailors found many uses for paracord other than shroud lines, and it became a staple utility item for all branches of the military. It is believed that soldiers stationed in the Middle East are the catalyst of the recent popularity of this great cord. As a sort of modern "trench art," paracord is tied into various useful items and accessories. The most common items are bracelets, given as gifts or sent home to loved ones.

Civilians wear these gift bracelets to show support for their friends and family in the military. They soon began to be marketed and worn as "survival bracelets" and advertised as a way to keep a necessary survival item at hand. These bracelets (as you will learn) are not only handy but also easy and fun to make.

The popularity of these bracelets encouraged manufacturers to develop and market commercial versions of paracord in many bright colors, color combinations, and sizes for the civilian market.

Working with paracord is easy and fun. You only need a handful of items and several lengths of cord to get started making tons of handy projects. This section introduces you to the tools you will need to make the projects in this book. You will also find some great tips and tricks to make working with paracord as simple as possible.

The Anatomy of Parachute Cord

Paracord consists of an outer jacket of nylon strands braided over inner strands of twisted nylon (called filler). The number of strands used for the jacket and the filler varies by the size of the cord. In 550 cord (the most common type), there are thirty-two strands in the jacket and seven or eight strands of filler.

Paracord is manufactured using technology that dates to the late nineteenth century. The nylon yarn is wound onto bobbins and then braided on a machine called a Maypole Braider. The largest builder of these braiding machines was the New England Butt Company of Providence, Rhode Island. Though they are no longer in business, the machines they built continue to braid cord around the clock.

Even though nylon is a synthetic fiber, it is still subject to variations in size and color with each batch. This means that cord braided on the same machines from different lots of yarn may vary in color, size, feel, and "shine."

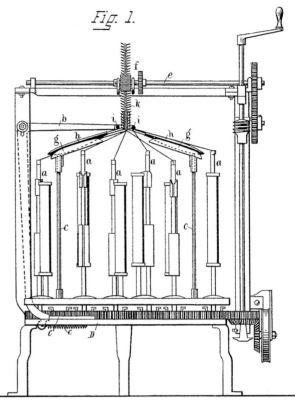

Figure 1. These illustrations are from an 1888 patent for improvements to braiding machines that were commonly used during that time.

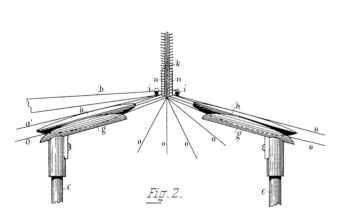

Figure 2. To braid the cord, bobbins wound with yarn are placed on carriers. A leather belt attached to a drive shaft moves the carriers, braiding the yarn around the filler strands.

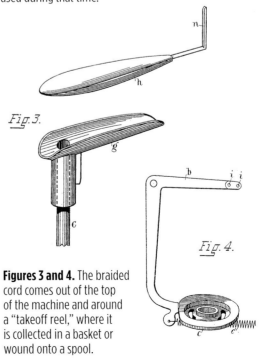

Figures 3 and 4. The braided cord comes out of the top of the machine and around a "takeoff reel," where it is collected in a basket or wound onto a spool.

Tools

Good sharp scissors, a butane lighter, and a yardstick or tape measure are all that you really need to start working with paracord. While these basic items will get you started, you'll find that the additional items listed below can often make projects a little bit easier and therefore more enjoyable to make.

Ⓐ QUALITY SCISSORS
Stiff and sharp blades are a necessity to cut paracord cleanly.

Ⓑ YARD STICK OR TAPE MEASURE
Most projects require several feet of paracord, so you'll want something longer than a standard ruler to measure it. You can also measure out marks on your workbench for quick reference.

Ⓒ BUTANE LIGHTER
This is used to fuse two lengths of cord together, as well as finish the ends to prevent unraveling.

Ⓓ BLACK PERMANENT MARKER.
This is good for marking lengths of cord, as well as touching up fused ends to make them look nicer.

Ⓔ CYANOACRYLATE GLUE.
Sold as "super glue," this adhesive can be used to secure cord ends and prevent fraying in projects where fusing is difficult.

Ⓕ FID
In its basic form, a fid is simply a pointed stick. This is used to work knots tighter as well as break them.

Ⓖ LACING NEEDLE
This is a metal tube that is pointed at one end and threaded on the inside at the other end. The threaded end can be twisted onto the end of a cord for weaving and tying knots. It can also be used in the same manner as a fid.

ABOUT METRIC

Throughout this book, you'll notice that every measurement is accompanied by a metric equivalent. Inches and feet are rounded off to the nearest half or whole centimeter unless precision is necessary. Please be aware that while this book will show 1 yard = 100 centimeters, the actual conversion is 1 yard = 90 centimeters, a difference of about 3 15/16" [10cm]. Using these conversions, you will always have a little bit of extra cord if measuring by the metric quantity.

H SPLICING TOOL

This is a metal loop set into a handle used for weaving cord ends back into knots or braids. A paperclip or piece of stiff wire bent into a U shape can be used in the same manner.

I PLIERS

Needle-nose pliers are useful for pulling knots tight.

J BINDER CLIPS

These are used to hold your spot when you have to stop in the middle of braiding.

K WINDERS

Winders will help you keep your cord organized and tangle free.

L C-CLAMPS

These handy tools allow you to make extra long pieces that are too big for a bracelet jig, such as the Utility Strap on page 24.

M BRACELET JIG

This simple tool makes tying bracelets super easy. Adding a screw hook to each end as shown increases the versatility of this tool.

N MONKEY'S FIST JIG

This simple jig makes monkey's fist knots easy. It's especially helpful when tying monkey's fist knots with two or more colors of cord.

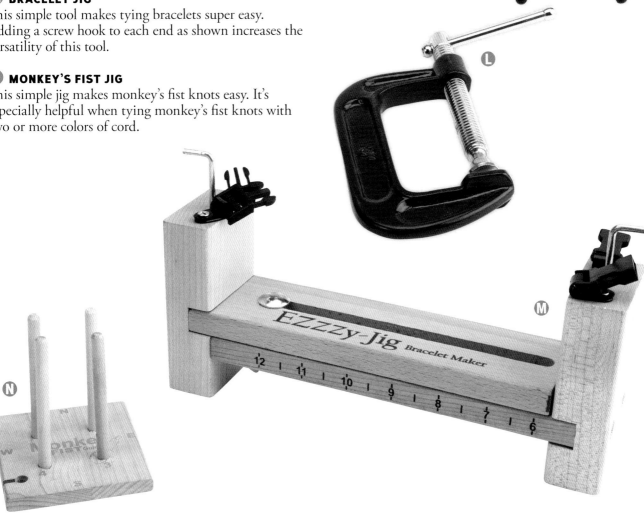

Tips and Techniques

What makes paracord great is how easy it is to work with. The tightly braided cord is smooth, yet slightly rough; it is incredibly strong with just enough elasticity. All of these elements make it a beautiful cord that knots very well. There are just a few techniques required for successfully working and crafting with parachute cord.

Stay organized. Commercial parachute cord is sold in small or large hanks, wound on spools, or around plastic frames. The spools and frames are easy to work with right away, as are the small hanks.

Larger hanks (50'–100' [15–30m]), however, can turn into a tangled mess.

When removing a large hank from its plastic bag, be careful to keep it intact. Locate the center of the hank and work your fingers all the way through it so it becomes a circular coil. Find the end of the outer loop and uncoil and cut the amount of cord needed for your project. Then secure the hank with a rubber band.

Locate the center of the hank and work your fingers all the way through it.

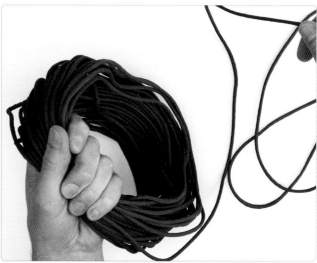

Uncoil the necessary amount of cord for your project.

Wind shorter lengths of cord around a piece of wood to form small hanks.

Wrap the shorter lengths of cord needed for your project into smaller hanks using a 3½" by 5½" (10 x 15cm) piece of stiff foam board or plywood. Secure the hanks with a rubber band. This keeps your cord neat and organized.

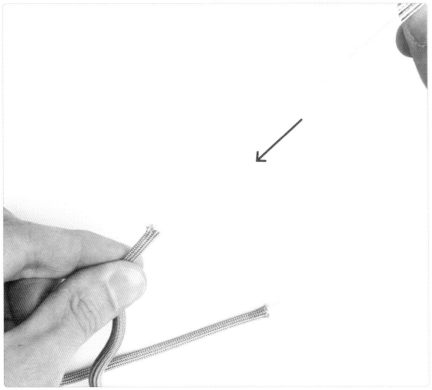

Hold on to the filler strands as you slide the casing off. Discard the filler strands and create your project using the casing only.

Smoothing the cord. During the manufacturing process, the filler strands in the cord might get twisted into bunches. When this happens, the cord will look lumpy or twisted, even when it has been shaken out. To remove these lumps and twists, cut a length of cord several inches longer than needed for your project. Tap your fingertip on the cut ends to expose the filler strands. Grasp the filler strands at each end of the cord and pull in opposite directions to smooth any lumps in the cord. Then pull the cord through your fingers to smooth out any twists. Finally, cut the ends square and fuse them (see page 8).

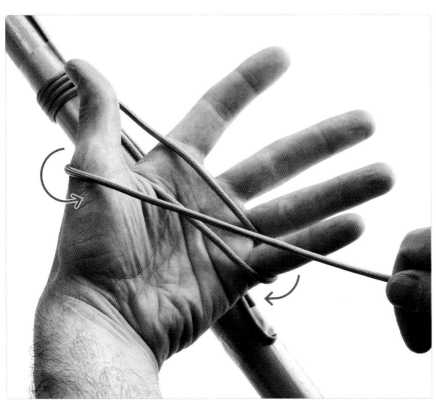

Wrap long lengths of cord in a figure eight pattern around your thumb and pinky, and then secure the cord with a rubber band.

Removing filler. Removing the filler and using only the casing will flatten the cord and make for flatter, tighter knots. To remove the filler, cut both ends of the cord. Tap one end to expose the filler strands. Grasp the filler strands and hold on to them as you pull the casing off. Fuse the ends flat (see page 8).

Bundling cord. Any time you will be working with a long length of cord in a project, form it into a bundle by wrapping it in a figure eight pattern around your thumb and pinky. Secure the bundle with a rubber band. Keep the bundle in place as you work so you can easily locate the working end and pull the cord through the knots. This will make knotting easier and faster, as you will not have to pull a long length of cord through your knot each time. Simply tug cord out of the bundle when you need more.

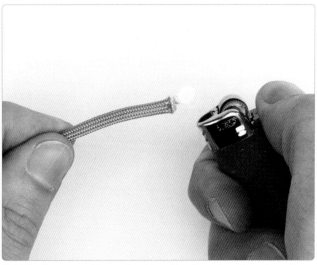

Hold the flame near the cord end to soften the nylon. Then shape it as desired using the side of your scissors.

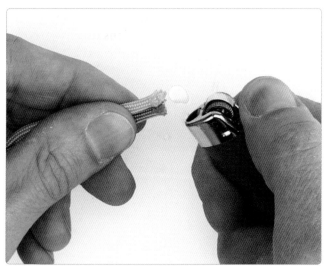

Hold the two cords you'd like to fuse parallel with ends even. Place the flame near the ends to soften them.

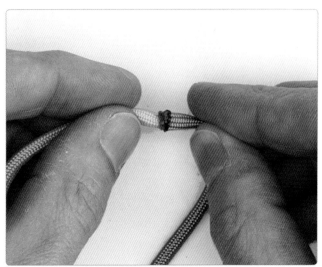

Pivot the cords and push the softened ends together. Hold them in place until the nylon cools.

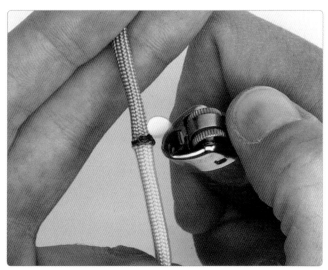

Place the flame near the fuse point and rotate the cord to soften it from all sides. Smooth and shape the softened fuse point with the side of your scissors.

Fusing the cord. Nylon is fusible, so it is easy to give your cord ends a nice clean finish. Caution and adult supervision should always be used around flames and heat. Work in a well-ventilated area. When possible, use exhaust fans or work outdoors. Exercise common sense and good judgment. When in doubt, always contact your local fire department for guidance.

For a professional-looking fused end, use a lighter to soften the nylon at the end of a cord. Never touch the flame to the cord; this poses a fire hazard and will scorch and blacken the cord. Once the nylon is softened, shape or flatten it using the smooth side of your scissors. Be careful—soft nylon is hot and can burn you. The fused ends of dark colored cords can be touched up with a black permanent marker.

To connect two pieces of cord, hold them parallel with ends even. Use a lighter to soften both ends at the same time. When both ends begin to soften, remove the flame and pivot the cords to bring the ends together. Push the ends together until the nylon cools. Gently reheat and smooth the fuse point with the side of your scissors.

Sometimes fusing cannot be done without damaging an adjacent cord or your project. In these cases, it is better to finish the cord ends using cyanoacrylate (super) glue with a brush-on applicator. Once the glue has dried, tuck the ends out of view.

Cord torsion. Torsion is distortion caused by applying torque in opposite directions to each end of an object. When applied to parachute cord, torsion can turn a nice straight length of cord into an unmanageable twisted mess.

Always be mindful of torsion when working with paracord. The very act of tying knots will cause the cord to turn and twist, so you must know when to twist or untwist the cord to achieve the nice, clean look you want. This is a skill only mastered with practice. When tying a knot, twist the cord to follow the loops. This is especially important in woven knots like the Turk's head or monkey's fist. With properly applied torsion, knots will hold well and look clean and even.

Length and type. The materials list for each project indicates the type of cord (550, 325, etc.) used to make the project. You can use any cord type you desire based on your personal preferences, as long as you make allowances for the change in diameter. All lengths listed are approximate, allowing plenty of extra to make working the various knots and weaves easier.

Cleaning the cord. Finished projects can be washed in cold or tepid water with very mild detergent. Use a soft brush to remove dirt and mud. The cord may shrink slightly after washing, but in most cases it can be stretched back to its original size.

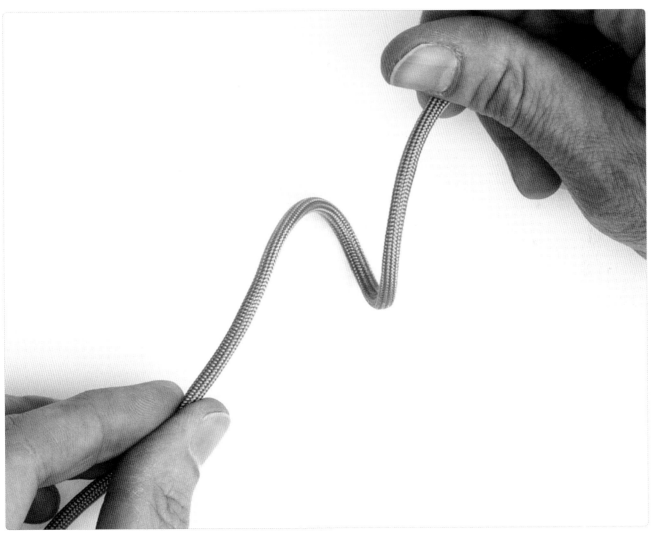

Torsion can build up in paracord and make for a lumpy knot. Be mindful of the way torsion builds up as you work, and twist or untwist the cord as necessary to ensure your knot work is nice and flat.

SURVIVAL BRACELET

Survival bracelets are a great and stylish way to carry extra cord. An average adult-sized bracelet contains six to eight feet of cord. Additionally, small items that could come in handy during an emergency can be knotted into the bracelet for later use. Identification, emergency contact info, and a small amount of cash are all useful things to consider knotting into your bracelet.

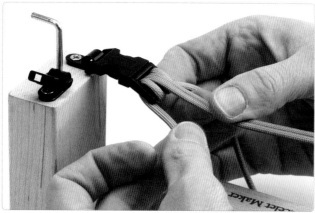

1 Fold the cord in half to form a loop at the center. Feed the loop through the end of a buckle and form a double lark's head knot (see page 31). Feed the working ends of the cord through the other end of the buckle, wrapping them around the buckle twice.

2 Use the working ends to form square knots (see page 35) over the strands stretched between the two buckle ends. You could also tie half hitch spiral knots (see page 37) for a spiral bracelet.

3 To finish, flip the bracelet over so the bottom is facing up. Loosen the loop of the last stitch and feed the lower working end through it to bring it to the center of the bracelet. Tighten the loop back down.

4 Trim the working ends. Tap the cut ends with your scissors until they become fuzzy. Then, use a lighter to soften the ends and flatten them with the side of your scissors.

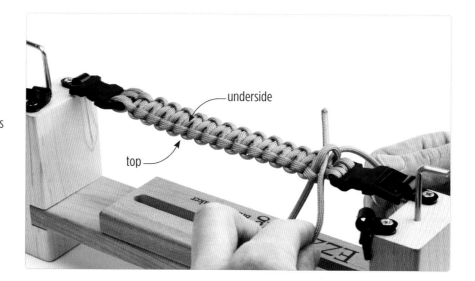

underside

top

TIP

A double lark's head knot fills the width of the buckle better than a single lark's head knot and makes for a nice finish.

MATERIALS
→ 8' (245cm) of 325 or 550 paracord
→ 12mm plastic buckle

Variations

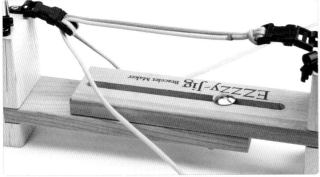

Two-color bracelet. To create a two-color bracelet, fuse two 4' (120cm) lengths of cord together (see page 8). Attach the cord to the buckle ends following step 1, making sure the fuse point is located between the two buckle ends. You will have two working ends in two different colors.

Hidden objects. Objects can be placed in the center of the bracelet and accessed later for use. For example, place a fishhook on top of the center strands and carefully tie knots over it with the working ends. For extra safety, cover any sharp objects with tape before tying them into the bracelet.

Compass. Attach a clip-on compass at the center of the bracelet. Tie square knots for about half the length of the bracelet. Then, slide the compass over all four strands. Continue tying square knots for the other half of the bracelet on the other side of the compass.

TIP

These bracelets are consumable. Don't be afraid to take them apart and use the cord when you need it. They're so easy and quick to make, you can have another one completed in minutes.

HIKING STICK GRIP

Fully customizable, the staff or hiking stick provides balance and stability when traveling on uneven ground. It can also be used to test wet and soft ground that would be a safety risk to walk on. By adding marks of measurement every foot, the staff can be used to check the depth of rivers or streams for crossing (fording). It can also be used as a tool of general measurement.

Creating a grip with paracord provides a sure grasp and is also a great way to carry extra cord. A wrist loop can be added to prevent dropping the staff. If desired, use brightly colored cord to increase your visibility for safety.

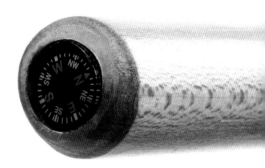

1 If desired, drill a hole in the top of the hiking stick about ¾" (2cm) wide and ¼" (0.5cm) deep. Use super glue to mount a compass in the hole.

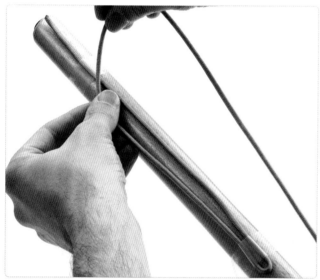

2 Form a loop on top of the hiking stick with the standing end of the 16' (490cm) strand and secure it in place using tape. For a 6"–7" (15–20cm) wrap, form a 7½" (20cm) loop about 4" (10cm) from the end of the stick.

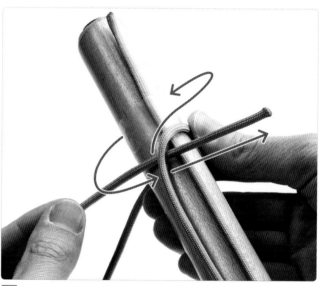

3 Bring the working end around the stick and under the left side of the loop formed by the standing end of the cord.

TIP

Make it easy to remember which direction you have to work in for alternating half hitching. Whichever side the cord comes out on, fold it back on itself and work in the opposite direction for the next knot.

4 Reverse the direction of the cord and form a half hitch (see pages 32 and 33).

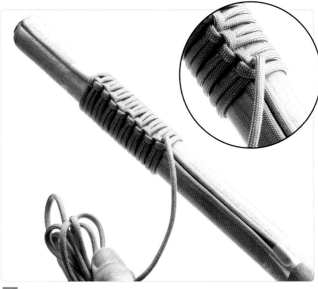

5 Work alternating half hitches (see page 33) around the stick over the loop formed by the standing end. Leave the bottom of the loop exposed. Form the seam of the alternating half hitches over the standing end loop to create a nice raised seam.

MATERIALS

→ 16' (490cm) of 550 paracord (for wrap)
→ 4'–5' (125–150cm) of 550 paracord (for wrist strap)
→ 4½' (135cm) of 325 paracord (for monkey's fist beads)
→ 16mm wood bead
→ Compass (optional)
→ Drill (optional)
→ Super glue (optional)
→ Tape
→ Paperclip

TIP

When bringing the working end through the bottom loop, feed it up through the loop (instead of down) to keep the end in line with the seam of the knots.

6 Remove the tape from the standing end. Bring the working end through the bottom loop. Then, pull on the standing end to bring the loop and working end flush against the alternating half hitch wrap. Pliers can be very helpful for this step. Trim and fuse the cord ends or finish them with glue.

7 Create a monkey's fist bead as described on page 41.

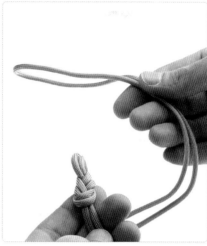

8 Tie a doubled figure eight knot as described on page 34, leaving a long loop.

9 Flatten out a paper clip and fold it in half around the loop of the figure eight knot. Feed the ends of the paper clip through the bead in the monkey's fist and use it to pull the loop of the figure eight knot through the bead. Use pliers to help with this step if necessary.

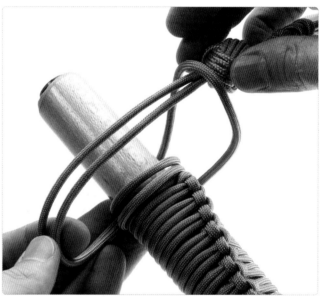

10 Use a double lark's head knot to attach the wrist strap to the hiking stick above the alternating half hitch wrap.

TIP

You can slide the loops of the knots around on the stick to fit your grip.

WRIST LANYARD

Any item or tool that is of value and importance can benefit from a wrist lanyard. Using a lanyard with items such as a compass or camera prevents loss and breakage from dropping. When attached to a tool or knife, it increases safety. A dropped knife or hammer is a hazard, especially when working in a tree or on a cliff.

1 Tie a lanyard knot as described on page 40 with the 4' (120cm) length of cord.

2 Find the center of the 3' (90cm) cord and place it over the bottom of the lanyard knot (inset). Use the four strands at the bottom of the knot to tie a crown knot round sinnet as described on page 36. For a square lanyard, tie crown knot square sinnets (see page 37).

3 Continue the crown knot round sinnet for about 1½" (5cm) or your desired length. Finish with a terminal knot as described on page 38. Trim and fuse or glue the ends, leaving about 1½" (5cm) tails.

4 Make a monkey's fist bead as described on page 41. Repeat step 9 for the Hiking Stick Grip (see page 14) to feed the lanyard loop through the monkey's fist bead.

MATERIALS
→ 4' (120cm) of 325 or 550 paracord
→ 3' (90cm) of 325 or 550 paracord
→ 4½' (135cm) of 325 paracord (for monkey's fist bead)
→ 16mm wood bead
→ Paperclip

CLASSIC NECK LANYARD

The neck lanyard is a classic and necessary piece of equipment. The concept is so simple that it is historically timeless. Neck lanyards as an exercise are a great way to show off knot work skill. Fully customizable, they are as individual as the maker.

The customizable length of this lanyard means it can be utilized for different applications. When worn around the neck, a whistle may be attached. This is used for distance communication and can also help rescuers locate your position in an emergency. Made to arm's length, a neck lanyard can be used to secure items to your belt to prevent loss during outdoor trips, which could mean the difference between life and death.

1 Working off of the snap hook, form a loose crown knot round sinnet as described on page 36. A hobby vice is incredibly helpful for this process.

2 Then, form a terminal knot as described on page 38. This creates a nice decorative knot at the base of the lanyard.

3 Work a four-strand round braid as described on page 45 for about 2' 8" (80cm).

4 With the filler removed, the cord will be very flat. Because of this, it is important to twist the cord and apply torsion as you work the braid. This way, the finished braid will be nice and smooth.

TIP

As you braid, the cord ends will become tangled. To untangle the ends, pick up one of the outside strands of the braid and pull it free. The remaining cord ends will also fall free.

PROJECTS

MATERIALS

→ Two 6' (185cm) lengths of
550 paracord, filler removed
→ 1 snap hook

5 Pair off the strands at the end of the braid with one strand of each color in each pair. Then, use them to tie an overhand knot at the end of the braid.

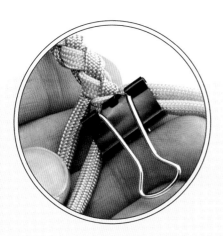

6 Work a crown knot round sinnet as described on page 36, leaving it very loose. Then feed about 3" (7cm) of the end of the lanyard through the center of the knot and tighten the knot around it. Continue tying crown knot round or square sinnets (see pages 36 and 37) around the lanyard for about 1" (2cm).

7 Make one final crown knot, leaving it loose, and form a terminal knot as described on page 38. Trim and fuse or glue the cord ends, leaving about a 1½" (5cm) tail on each. The crown knots will slide along the length of the lanyard, making it adjustable.

TIP

If you have to leave your project in the middle of braiding, use a binder clip to hold the strands in place until you're ready to start working again.

BREAKAWAY LANYARD

This lanyard includes two hooks so multiple items can be attached to it. The breakaway buckle brings an added level of safety, as the lanyard will come apart if it gets caught on something, preventing injury.

1 Repeat steps 1–2 of the Classic Lanyard (see page 16) to form a terminal knot off of a snap hook using two of the 4½' (135cm) strands. Work a four-strand round braid as described on page 45 for 1½' (45cm).

2 Follow the instructions on page 45 to attach one half of the breakaway buckle to the end of the braid and weave the cord ends back into the braid. Trim and fuse or glue the cord ends to finish.

3 Repeat steps 1–2 to form the second half of the lanyard.

4 Tie a Turk's head knot on your fingers as described on page 43. Feed both ends of the lanyard through the knot and tighten it around the lanyard. This forms a sliding knot around the lanyard to make it adjustable. Trim and fuse or glue the cord ends of the Turk's head knot.

MATERIALS

→ Four 4½' (135cm) lengths of 95 paracord (for lanyard)
→ 3½' (105cm) of 325 paracord (for Turk's head knot)
→ 2 snap hooks
→ 5mm plastic breakaway buckle
→ Splicing tool

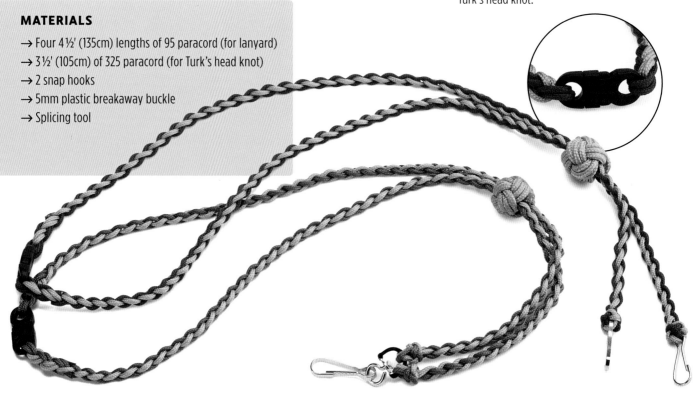

WATER BOTTLE HOLDER

Water is an essential for any hiking or camping trip, and a water bottle holder gives you a hands-free way to carry it. The rings at the top of the holder allow it to be attached to a backpack or suspended from a tent ceiling. If you're out for a short hike and want to travel light, the shoulder strap gives you the option of carrying a water bottle without a backpack.

1 Fold each cord in half and attach them all to one ring using lark's head knots.

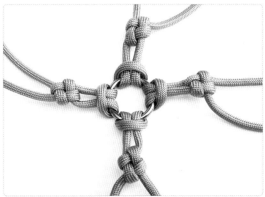

2 Place your water bottle on top of the ring to determine where you want to tie your crown knots. You want them to be positioned about halfway between the ring and the edge of the bottle to form a stable base. Use each pair of strands to tie a crown knot for netting as described on page 39.

MATERIALS

→ Four 6' (185cm) lengths of 325 or 550 paracord
→ Three 1" (25mm) rings

3 Form an alternating set of crown knots around the bottle. To do this, take one strand each from two adjacent crown knots and use them to tie a crown knot. Repeat with the remaining strands around, spacing the knots evenly.

4 Continue to tie alternating crown knots around the bottle until you have formed a net that reaches to the top edge.

5 Take one strand each from two adjacent crown knots. Feed the ends through a ring, positioning it about 2" (5cm) from the edge of the water bottle. Tie two square knots back over the strands with the working ends. Trim and fuse the ends.

6 Working counterclockwise, repeat with the next two strands, tying them onto the same ring. Repeat steps 5–6 on the other side of the water bottle with a second ring.

7 For the shoulder strap, tie a four-strand round braid (see page 45) off of a carabiner. Work the braid for about 4' (120cm). Follow the instructions on page 45 to attach other end of the braid to the carabiner and weave the cord ends back into the braid. Trim and fuse or glue the cord ends to finish.

TIP

Use a ruler to help keep your knotting even. Place the top edge below the first knot, and tie your second knot against the bottom edge.

WATCH STRAP

Many people venture into the outdoors to escape the constraints of time, but wearing a watch is useful for keeping track of daylight and distance traveled when hiking. A watch can also be used as a makeshift compass.

This watch strap allows you to replace a broken band on a watch you already own. It's also a great way to create a custom piece that shows off your individuality and knot skill.

1 Fold one strand in half and use it to tie a lark's head knot around the tine of the buckle. Fold the other two straps in half over the buckle on either side of the tine.

2 Work a six-strand braid as described on page 46 for about 9½" (25cm). As you braid, keep all the strands flat rather than twisting them as for the four-strand round braid. Otherwise, the finished piece will twist.

MATERIALS

- → Three 4' (120cm) lengths of 550 paracord, filler removed
- → ¾" (20mm) strap buckle
- → 1 watch face with removable strap pins
- → Splicing tool

3 To finish the end of the braid, fold the right center strand up to the left.

4 Then begin weaving the ends back into the braid using a splicing tool. Start with the second from left strand. Then weave in the far left strand.

5 Continue with the far right strand.

6 Flip the strap over so you are working on the back side. Fold the right center strand up to the left. Weave in the left center strand. Then, trim and fuse or glue the cord ends.

7 Attach the watch face by removing the pins, placing the strap on the back of the watch face, and replacing the pins.

TIP

Keep even tension as you work to avoid pulling the project to one side or the other, creating a zigzag shape.

BEDROLL STRAPS AND HANDLE

When using the improvised version, a bedroll is a great way to bundle and carry items in an emergency situation. This method of tying up a bundle is also a good way to pack a tent, tarp, or ground cloth.

In the permanent arrangement, using a bedroll strap makes easy work of storing and carrying clothing and sleeping gear. Comfort and a good night's rest are immensely important to outdoor life.

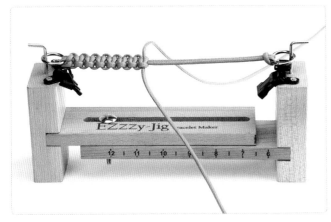

1 For the straps, follow steps 1–6 for the Watch Strap to make two braided straps 4' (120cm) long.

2 For the handle, follow steps 1–4 for the survival bracelet (see page 10) to make an 8" (20cm)-long handle using ¾" (20mm) rings instead of buckles. Use a single lark's head knot to attach the cord to the first ring and only wrap the cords once around the second ring instead of twice (see the photo at the left).

3 Feed the braided straps through the rings at the ends of the handle when you are ready to secure them around your bedroll.

MATERIALS

→ 12' (365cm) of 550 paracord (for handle)
→ Six 12' (365cm) lengths of 550 paracord, filler removed (for straps)
→ Two ¾" (20mm) strap buckles
→ Splicing tool

UTILITY STRAP

Made to be adjustable, this handy strap is incredibly versatile and can be attached to any bag you want. The strong cord makes it an excellent replacement for a broken duffle or satchel strap. It can also be used in conjunction with the Bedroll Straps and Handle (see page 23). It's an excellent way to keep a lot of cord at hand.

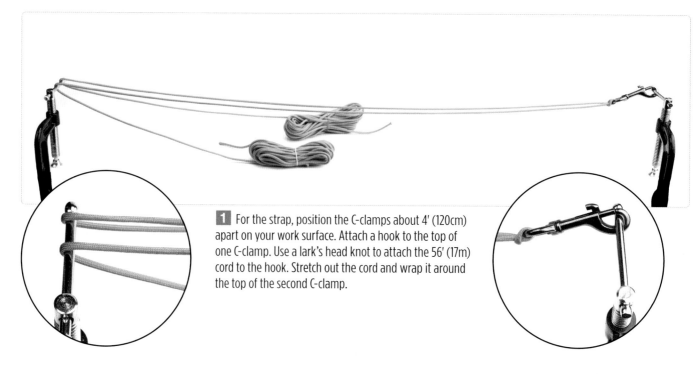

1 For the strap, position the C-clamps about 4' (120cm) apart on your work surface. Attach a hook to the top of one C-clamp. Use a lark's head knot to attach the 56' (17m) cord to the hook. Stretch out the cord and wrap it around the top of the second C-clamp.

2 Form the working ends into bundles as described on page 7 and secure them with rubber bands. Use the working ends to tie square knots over the strands stretched between the C-clamps.

3 For the shoulder pad, hold the ends of the three 8' (245cm) strands of paracord parallel and fuse them together. Work a three-strand hair braid (see page 44) until you reach the opposite end of the cords. Fuse the ends of the cords together as before.

4 Use the braided strand to tie square knots (see page 35) over the strap to form an adjustable shoulder pad. Because the hair braid is a flat braid, do not twist the strands as you tie the square knots to keep everything flat.

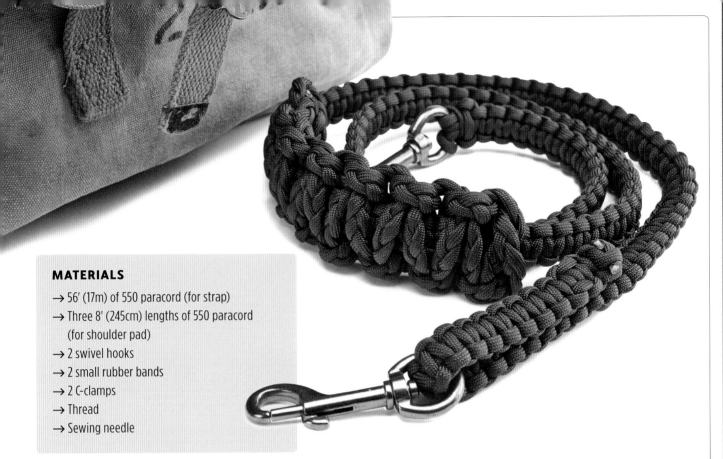

MATERIALS

→ 56' (17m) of 550 paracord (for strap)
→ Three 8' (245cm) lengths of 550 paracord (for shoulder pad)
→ 2 swivel hooks
→ 2 small rubber bands
→ 2 C-clamps
→ Thread
→ Sewing needle

5 Repeat step 3 from the Survival Bracelet (page 10) to secure the ends on the underside of the shoulder pad.

6 Stitch the working ends in place on the underside of the shoulder pad. Then trim and fuse or glue the ends.

7 Slide the second hook onto the loose end of the strap, positioning it where desired to set the length of the strap. Fold back the end of the strap and use an additional piece of cord and a lacing needle to stitch the fold in place. Use a fid to open up the loops at the edges of the knots and feed the lacing needle through. Tie the ends of the lacing strand together in a square knot on the underside of the strap. Trim and fuse or glue the ends.

BELT

Besides their usual application of holding up pants, belts have many uses in the outdoors. A strong belt can be used to carry gear that needs to be readily accessible. It provides a place to attach lanyards holding useful items. A belt can also be used in an emergency as a sling or to pull someone out of mud or water.

1 Fold one strand in half and tie it around the tine of the buckle using a lark's head knot. Fold the remaining cords in half around the buckle, placing two on each side of the buckle tine.

2 Work a ten-strand braid as described on pages 47 and 48 for 4' (120cm) or the desired length.

3 Turn the belt over so the underside is facing up. Fold the right center strand up to the left.

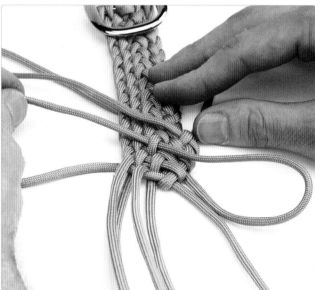

4 Weave the remaining cord ends back into the braid using a splicing tool, starting with the fourth from left strand. Then weave in the second from left strand.

5 Flip the belt over so the top side is facing up. Continue to weave in the remaining cord ends, starting with the top two right strands.

6 Fold the center right strand up to the left. Weave in the bottom left strand.

7 At this point, you are able to trim and fuse or glue the cord ends. You can continue weaving in the remaining ends if desired, but this can make the belt end very bulky.

MATERIALS
→ Five 12' (265cm) lengths of 550 paracord
→ 1¼" (30mm) frame buckle
→ Splicing tool

TIP

If using a dark colored cord, touch up the cord ends with a permanent marker after fusing.

MONKEY'S FIST KEYCHAIN

The monkey's fist knot was originally used nautically to add weight to the end of a rope to make it easier to throw. This application is useful for hanging "bear bags" (food bags) and clothes lines, rigging shelters, or performing rescues. The monkey's fist makes a great decorative key fob. Using a closed cell foam core creates a float that can prevent loss of keys in water.

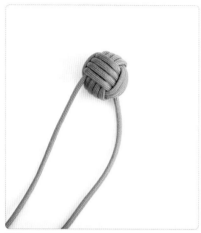

1 Follow the instructions on pages 41–42 to create a single color or tri-color monkey's fist.

2 Follow the instructions on page 42 to tie a wrapping knot with the standing end and working end. Attach a key ring to the top loop of the wrapping knot.

MATERIALS

For single color:
→ 4 ½' (135cm) of 550 paracord
→ 20mm wood bead
→ Key ring

For tri-color:
→ 3' (90cm) each of 3 colors of 550 paracord
→ 20mm wood bead
→ Key ring

For beads:
→ 4 ½' (135cm) of 325 paracord
→ 1' (30cm) of 325 paracord in a contrasting color
→ 16mm wood bead

TIP

Create a float using a 1" (2cm) foam cube as the center of the monkey's fist and 9' (275cm) of cord.

FLASHLIGHT WRAP

Modern flashlights are often made of metal, which can become slick due to sweaty hands or damp weather. Wrapping a flashlight with parachute cord creates a comfortable and secure grip. Using brightly colored cord makes the flashlight easier to find in a backpack or when set down. The wrapped grip can also cushion the flashlight, helping to prevent damage if it is dropped.

1 Form a loop on top of the flashlight with the standing end of the 6' (185cm) strand and secure it in place using tape.

2 Bring the working end around the flashlight and under the right side of the loop formed by the standing end of the cord.

MATERIALS
→ 6' (185cm) of 95 paracord (for wrap)
→ Two 4' (120cm) lengths of 95 paracord (for Turk's head knots)
→ Tape

  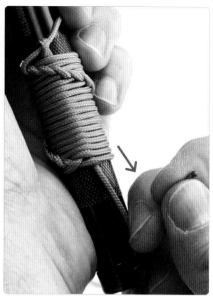

3 Work half hitches (see page 32) around the flashlight over the loop formed by the standing end. Leave the top of the loop exposed.

4 Remove the tape from the standing end. Bring the working end through the top loop.

5 Then, pull on the standing end to bring the loop and working end flush against the half hitch wrap. Trim and fuse the cord ends or finish them with glue.

6 Tie a Turk's head knot around your fingers as described on page 43.

7 Slide the knot from your fingers onto the flashlight and tighten it around the flashlight. A fid can be helpful for this process. Trim the ends and fuse or glue them to finish. Tuck them behind the knot to hide them.

8 Add a second Turk's head knot on the other side of the half hitch wrap.

TIP

If wrapping a larger flashlight, use 9' [275cm] of 95 cord for the wrap and 6' [185cm] of 95 cord for each Turk's head knot.

Knot work is a wonderful way to produce custom items that show off your skill and individuality. This section will introduce you to all of the knots used to make the projects in this book. While some knots might require more practice than others to master, all are very achievable. Furthermore, these knots can be used for any number of applications outside of the projects shown here. Use your creativity to put them together in different combinations to see what you can make.

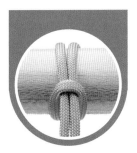

LARK'S HEAD KNOT

DOUBLE LARK'S HEAD KNOT

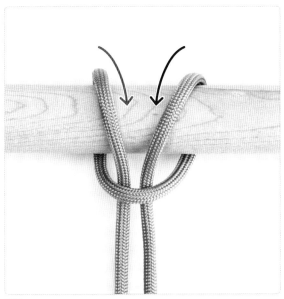

1 Form a loop at the center of the cord and then bring the cord ends through it.

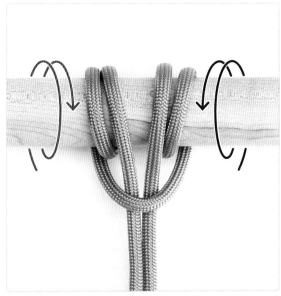

1 Form a lark's head knot and then bring the cord ends around the form and through the loop a second time.

TIP

Create shoelaces by fusing aglets onto each end of a cord.

HALF HITCH

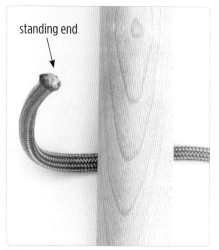

standing end

1 Place the cord under your form with the standing end to the left and the working end to the right.

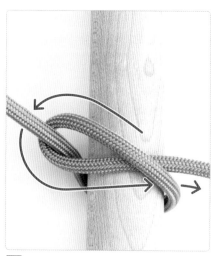

2 Bring the working end around the standing end and through the loop formed in the cord.

3 Working below the previous knot, bring the working end around the form and cross it underneath itself, forming a loop around the form. Tighten.

4 Repeat, bringing the working end around the form and crossing it underneath itself.

5 Half hitch repeated.

ALTERNATING HALF HITCH

1 Repeat steps 1–2 for the half hitch (see page 32).

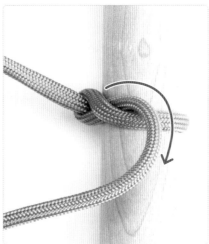

2 Reverse the direction of the cord by bringing the working end out to the left side of the form.

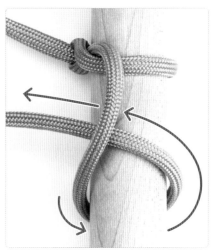

3 Form a half hitch by bringing the working end around the form and through the loop formed by the cord.

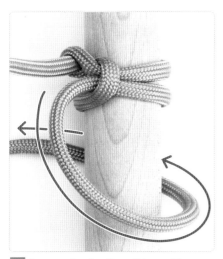

4 Reverse the direction of the cord by bringing the working end out to the right side of the form and around the form.

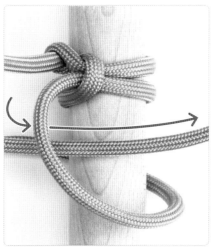

5 Form a half hitch by bringing the working end through the loop formed by the cord.

6 Alternating half hitch repeated.

FIGURE EIGHT KNOT

1 Start with the cord laid out flat. The top end is the working end.

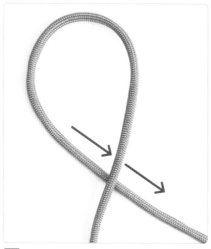

2 Bring the working end down around and under the cord to form a loop.

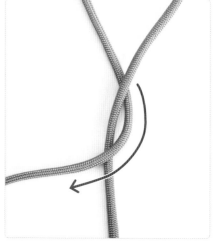

3 Bring the working end across the cord to the left.

Doubling the Knot

Ⓐ You can double the knot by following it through with the standing end. Fold the standing end back on itself to form a loop at the base of the knot. The size of the loop you make will depend on your project. Then, feed the standing end through the knot, always keeping it parallel and to the right of the knot cord. Be mindful of torsion and twist or untwist the cord as necessary so everything lies flat.

Ⓑ Tighten.

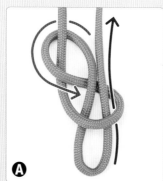
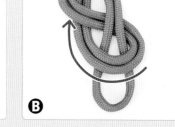

Ⓐ You can also double the knot by doubling up the cord used to tie it. Fold the cord in half to form a loop at the center and use the loop as the working end.

Ⓑ Tighten.

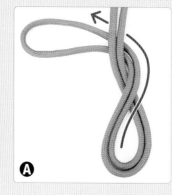
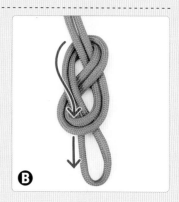

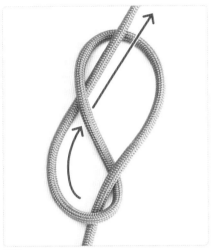

4 Bring the working end under and then through the loop.

5 Tighten.

SQUARE KNOT OVER FILLER

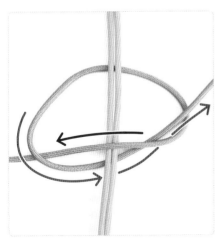

1 Start with the working cord behind and perpendicular to the filler cords. Bring the right working end over the filler cords. Bring the left working end over the right working end, under the filler cords, and over and through the loop formed by the right working end.

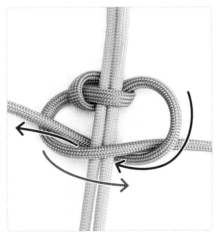

2 Bring the left working end over the filler cords. Bring the right working end over the left working end, under the filler cords, and over and through the loop formed by the left working end.

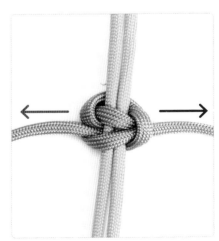

3 Tighten.

CROWN KNOT ROUND SINNET

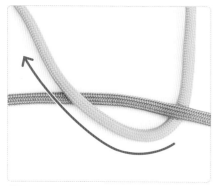

1 Arrange two cords perpendicular to one another to form a + shape with the vertical cord on the bottom. Working clockwise, fold the bottom strand up to the left. If this is your first time making this knot, it might help to tape each strand down after you fold it.

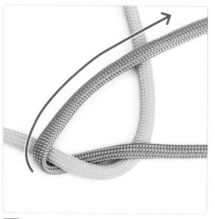

2 Fold the left strand over to the right.

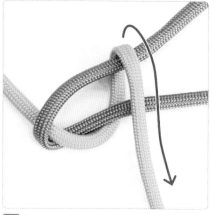

3 Fold top strand down to the right.

4 Fold the right strand over to the left and feed it through the loop at the bottom left of the knot formed by the first fold you made.

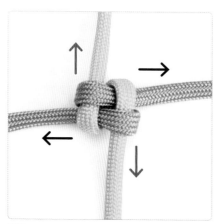

5 Tighten, being careful to pull each strand evenly and at right angles to the strands next to it to form a square as shown.

6 Repeating the pattern makes a round sinnet of crown knots.

CROWN KNOT SQUARE SINNET

1 Working clockwise, repeat steps 1–5 for the Crown Knot Round Sinnet (see page 36).

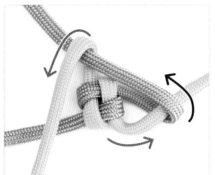

2 To create the square shape, reverse the knotting pattern by working counter clockwise. Start by folding the bottom strand up to the right. Fold the right strand over to the left. Fold the top strand down to the left. Finish by folding the left strand over to the right and feeding it through the loop at the bottom right of the knot formed by the first fold you made (not shown).

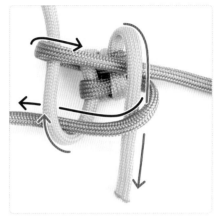

3 Reverse the knotting pattern again, working clockwise. Repeat, alternating between clockwise and counterclockwise.

HALF HITCH SPIRAL

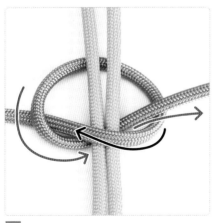

1 Start with the working cord behind and perpendicular to the filler cords. Bring the right working end over the filler cords. Bring the left working end over the right working end, under the filler cords, and over and through the loop formed by the right working end.

2 Repeat.

3 As you repeat the knotting pattern, the working cords will form a spiral around the filler cords.

TERMINAL KNOT

1 After working a Crown Knot Sinnet for the desired length, repeat steps 1–4 for the Crown Knot Round Sinnet (see page 36) to form a loose crown knot.

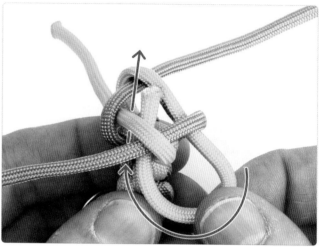

2 Continue working in the direction (clockwise or counterclockwise) you did to form the crown knot. Starting with the bottom strand, bring it around the adjacent loop and feed it up through the center of the knot.

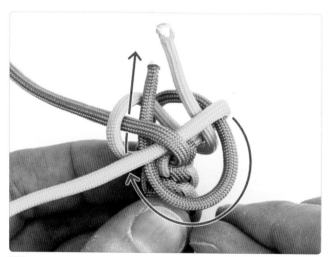

3 Rotate the knot and continue until all strands have been fed up through the center of the knot.

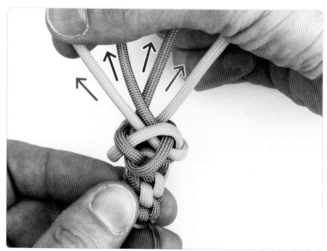

4 To work the knot tight, pull up on the ends, working clockwise. As the knot grows tighter, you can pull on all the ends at once to finish.

CROWN KNOT FOR NETTING

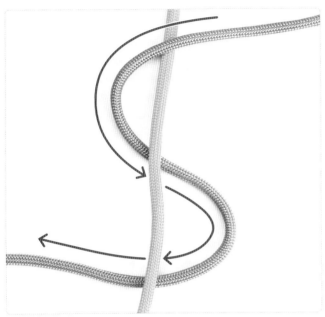

1 Start with two cords parallel to one another. Cross the bottom end of cord A (the right cord) over cord B (the left cord). Then, use cord A to pull a loop underneath cord B, to the right.

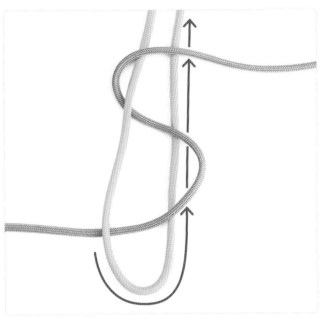

2 Fold the bottom of cord B up to the right, passing it behind cord A at all three intersections.

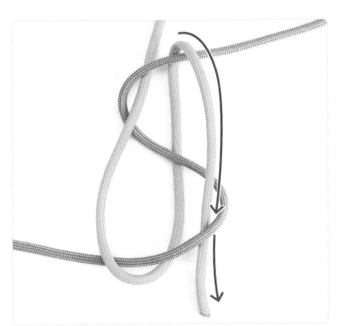

3 Fold the top right strand of cord B down over the top right strand of cord A and down through the bottom loop formed by cord A (the loop you created in step 1).

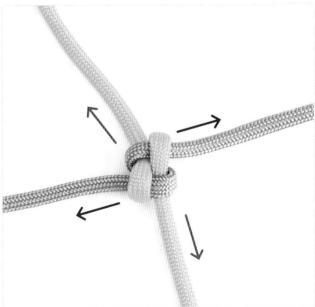

4 Tighten, being careful to pull each strand evenly and at right angles to the strands next to it to form a square as shown.

LANYARD KNOT

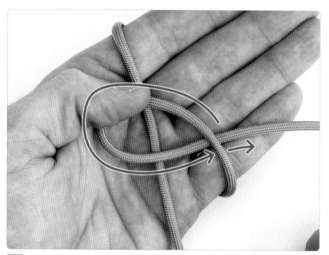

1 Fold the cord in half over your fingers with the left working end in front of your hand and the right working end behind your hand. Use the right working end to form a loop and position it on top of the left working end. Make sure the right working end is under the loop as shown and not on top.

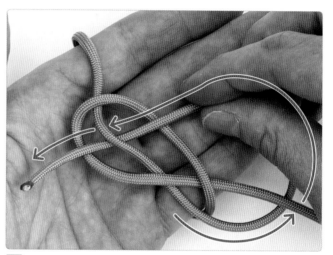

2 Bring the left working end under the right working end, and then feed it through the strands on top of your hand, going over, under, over.

3 Bring the right working end over the strand looped around the top of your hand and up through the center of the knot.

4 Bring the left working end over the strand looped around the bottom of your hand and up through the center of the knot.

5 Remove the knot from your hand. Work it tight by pulling up on the working ends and down on the starting loop. Work each section of the knot individually as necessary.

TIP

Lanyard knots make excellent zipper pulls. Feed the cord through the zipper and then tie the lanyard knot, keeping the zipper in the loop of the knot. You can also turn the knot into a button by working the starting loop down into the knot.

MONKEY'S FIST

Use about 4 ½'–5' (135–150cm) to practice this. A lacing needle makes it easier to form the knot.

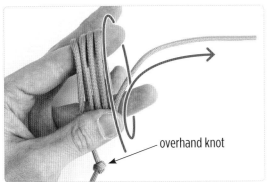

overhand knot

1 Tie an overhand knot in the standing end as a point of reference. Make four wraps around your fingers with the working end, keeping the wraps parallel at all times. The number of wraps will depend on the size of the core. Make more or fewer wraps as required. Remove your middle finger from the center of the wraps and bring the working end out to the right.

2 Use the working end to make four horizontal wraps over the center point of the vertical wraps, making sure the wraps are all parallel and do not cross at any time. Bring the working end out to the right.

3 Place the core ball in the center of the wraps.

4 Bring the working end through the vertical wraps out to the left side. Then, working within (underneath) the vertical wraps and over top of the horizontal wraps, make four vertical wraps around the core ball, keeping all the wraps parallel.

5 Remove the knot from your fingers. To work the knot tight, start at the standing end and tug on the cord gently to pull up a loop. Continue to tug on the cord to work this loop all the way through the knot. This slowly tightens the knot around the core ball.

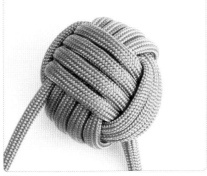

6 Repeat, starting from the working end to pull up a loop and pull the cord back through the knot, slowly tightening it around the core ball. Repeat as many times as necessary to tighten the knot around the core ball as desired.

Monkey's Fist Bead

A Tie a monkey's fist knot over a wooden bead. Keep the knot fairly loose, and then locate the openings in the bead.

B Feed a cord through the bead in the monkey's fist. Work the knot tight around the bead. Then trim and fuse the cord ends of the monkey's fist instead of finishing them with a wrapping knot (see page 42. Set the monkey's fist bead aside for use in your project later.

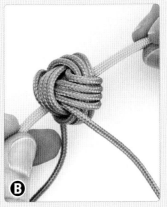

Tri-Color Monkey's Fist

A Hold the ends of two 2' (60cm) strands in two different colors together and fuse them in place.

B Make two vertical wraps around your fingers with the fused cords side by side. Then, place the core ball between the wraps. Bring the working end of the fused cords out to the left between the vertical wraps.

C Make two horizontal wraps around the core ball, over the center point of the vertical wraps.

D Then, working within (underneath) the vertical wraps and over the horizontal wraps, make four vertical wraps with a 3' (90cm) cord in a third color.

E Begin working the knot tight around the core ball. When working the 2' (60cm) strands, treat the two parallel strands as if they were one.

F Trim and fuse all cord ends except the ends of the 3' (90cm) strand. Use the two ends to form a wrap as described below.

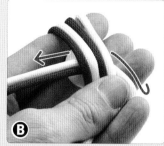

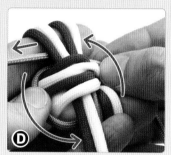

Finishing with a Wrapping Knot

A Use the working end to make a loop on top of the standing end as shown.

B Pinch all the cords together near the center of the loop. Then take the standing end and wrap it around the loop and the working end, leaving a bit of the loop exposed at the top. Keep wrapping toward the ball until you reach the bottom of the loop; feed the standing end through the bottom of the loop.

C Pull on the working end to bring the bottom loop with the standing end up against the wraps. Trim and fuse the cord ends. Use the top loop to attach the monkey's fist to a key ring or other object.

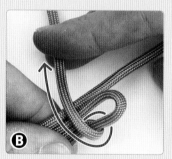

TURK'S HEAD KNOT

Use about 4½'–5' (135–150cm) to practice this knot.

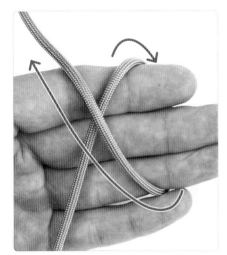

1 Place the standing end across your palm. Then, bring the working end around your hand and cross it over the standing end, forming an X. The working end will be at the top left of the X. If desired, wrap the cord around your first three fingers only so you can hold the bottom of the cords in place with your pinky.

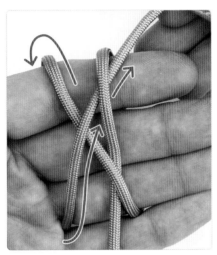

2 Bring the working end around your hand, over the top left leg of the X, and then under the top right leg of the X.

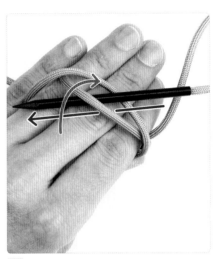

3 Turn your hand over so you are looking at the back. You will see two parallel strands. Cross the left strand over the right. This will form an oval shape. Bring the working end through the oval, going over the right side and under the left side.

standing end

4 Flip your hand over so you are looking at your palm. Find the standing end and follow it through the knot with the working end, always keeping the working end to the right of the standing end.

5 Continue to follow the knot through with the working end, always keeping the working end to the right of the strand you are following.

6 Continue building the knot to the right until you have made three passes. Both ends of the cord will terminate at the same location on opposite sides of the knot, which creates the continuous look. Repeat steps 5–6 of the monkey's fist knot (see page 41) to work the knot tight. Trim and fuse the ends of the cord on the underside of the knot.

THREE-STRAND HAIR BRAID

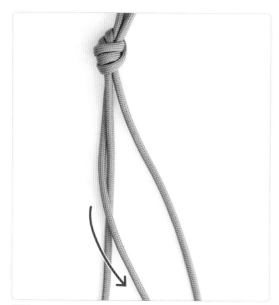

1 Cross the left strand over the center strand.

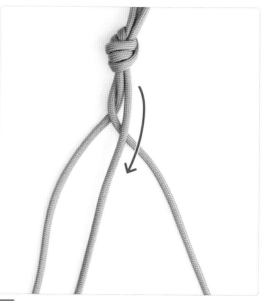

2 Cross the right strand over the new center strand.

3 Repeat, crossing each strand into the center, alternating between left and right sides.

TIP

If you forget which side you should be working on, remember that you will always work the highest strand.

FOUR-STRAND ROUND BRAID

Attaching Objects and Weaving in Ends

Ⓐ Cross two opposing cords over the center of the braid.

Ⓑ Place the object you're attaching to the braid over the crossed cords. Cross the two remaining cords over the center of the braid, feeding them through the object you're attaching to the braid.

Ⓒ Use the splicing tool to weave the cord ends back through the braid, following the braiding pattern. Start with the two cords threaded through the object you're attaching to the braid.

Ⓓ Repeat until all the cord ends have been woven back into the braid for an inch or two. Then trim and fuse or glue the cord ends.

1 Fold two cords in half over the item you are braiding onto, such as a split ring. Arrange the strands so those of the same color are next to each other. This will create vertical stripes in the finished braid.

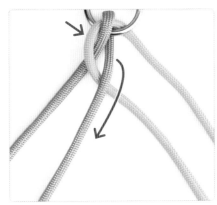

2 Bring the far left strand under the two strands in the center and back over one to the left (this will be the rightmost of the strands you just crossed under).

3 Bring the far right strand under the two strands in the center and back over one to the right (the leftmost of the strands you just crossed under).

4 Continue the pattern, alternating between left and right sides.

Ⓐ

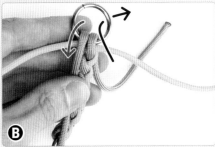
Ⓑ

Ⓒ

Ⓓ

TIP

Arranging the strands so the colors alternate will create spiral stripes in the finished braid.

SIX-STRAND FLAT BRAID

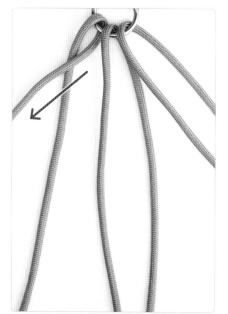

1 Fold three cords in half over the item you are braiding onto, such as a split ring. Bring the second from left strand over the far left strand.

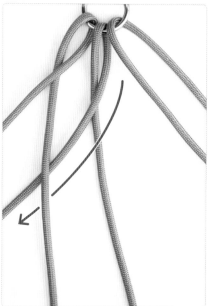

2 Bring the fourth from left strand over one and under one, working toward the left.

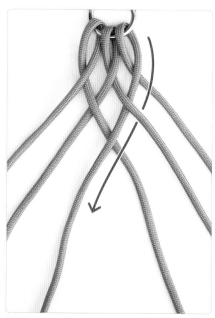

3 Bring the far right strand over one, under one, and over one, working toward the center.

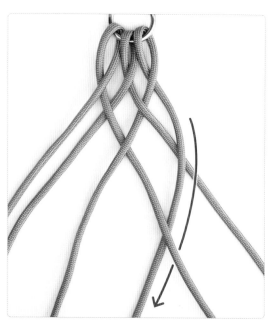

4 Bring the far right strand over one and under one, working toward the center.

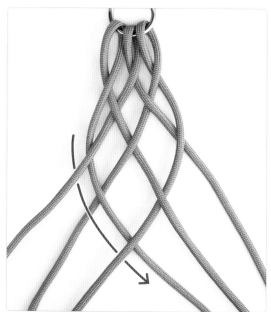

5 Bring the far left strand under one, over one, and under one, working toward the center. Repeat steps 4–5 for the length of the braid.

KNOTS

TEN-STRAND FLAT BRAID

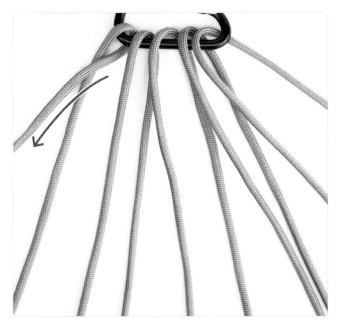

1 Fold five cords in half over the item you are braiding onto, such as a carabiner. Bring the second from left strand over the far left strand.

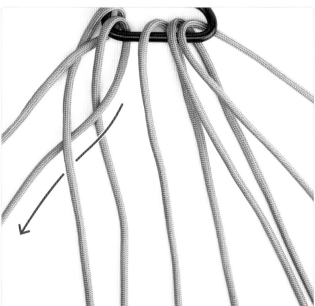

2 Bring the fourth from left strand over one and under one, working toward the left.

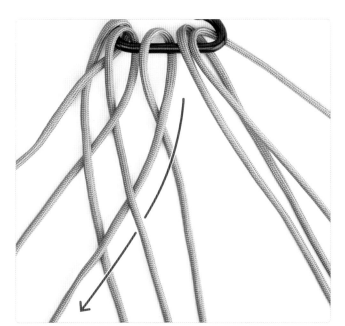

3 Bring the sixth from left strand over one, under one, and over one, working toward the left.

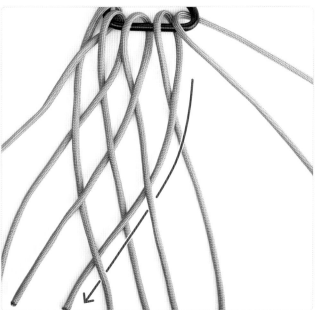

4 Bring the eighth from left strand over one, under one, over one, and under one, working toward the left.

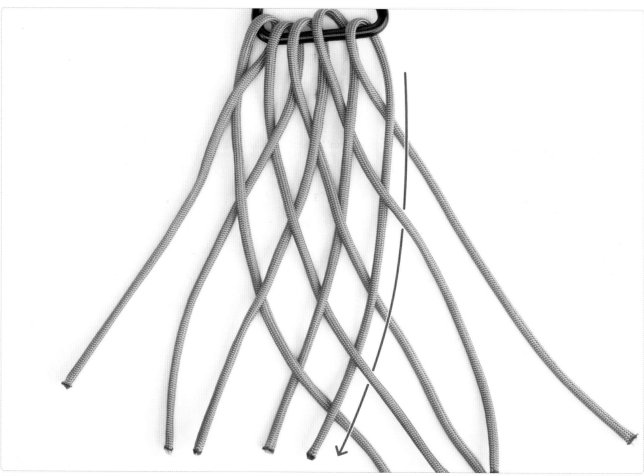

5 Bring the far right strand over one, under one, over one, under one, and over one, working toward the left.

6 Bring the far right strand over one, under one, over one, and under one, working toward the center.

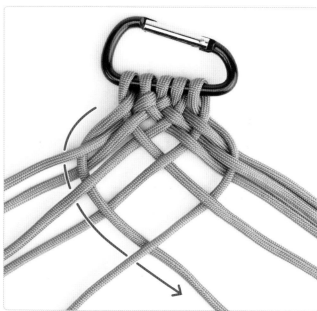

7 Bring the far left strand under one, over one, under one, over one, and under one working toward the center. Repeat steps 6–7 for the length of the braid.